FISH

....

AND

....

SHIPS

....

First published in 2023 by the National Maritime Museum, Park Row,
Greenwich, London SE10 9NF

ISBN: 978-1-906367-76-3

At the heart of the UNESCO World Heritage Site of Maritime Greenwich
are the four world-class attractions of Royal Museums Greenwich –
the National Maritime Museum, the Royal Observatory, the Queen's
House and *Cutty Sark*.

www.rmg.co.uk

A CIP catalogue record for this book is available from the British Library.

Image credits: p.45, Naci Yavuz; p.60, Uncle Leo; pp. 62, 87, Natata; p.69,
Ecaterina Sciuchina. Courtesy of shutterstock.com.

Design by Matt Windsor.
Typesetting by Thomas Bohm, User Design, Illustration and Typesetting.
Printed and bound in the UK by TJ Books.

10 9 8 7 6 5 4 3 2 1

FISH

. . . .

AND

. . . .

SHIPS

. . . .

A Nautical Miscellany

NATIONAL
MARITIME MUSEUM
GREENWICH

THE
NAUTICAL
WORLD

· · · · · · · · · · · · · · · ·

Three quarters of all the countries in the world have a coastline. Access to the oceans defines many nations and has influenced their histories for thousands of years. For some, the sea has been an excellent line of defence, for others it has left them open to constant attack. Some small island states have produced the most adventurous explorers while others have made themselves centres of trade.

Despite so many lives revolving around the seas for so long, we know more about the surface of the Moon than we do the ocean floor. On average the seabed is only a couple of miles below the waves, but the mysteries of the deep continue to fascinate, mystify and scare even the most landlocked landlubber. This book explores the ships, the explorers and the voyages that have revealed so much about the world beyond the shore.

WHEN IS A BOAT NOT A SHIP?

....

Unsurprisingly, the answer is not very clear-cut and, to add to the complication, the historical development of these terms and the vessels themselves needs to be taken into account.

Starting with a boat, a common definition is that it can be carried on a ship. But a ship carried on a shipcarrier does not become a boat... A boat is sometimes defined as a small open craft without any deck and propelled by oars, an outboard engine or small sails. A submarine, however, is always referred to as a boat, despite being substantially larger than a typical boat, as are

COPPER BOTTOMED
Today it is used to describe something that is very stable or safe. It comes from copperbottomed ships, which were fitted with copper plating on the underside of their hulls to protect the wooden planking.

fishing boats, which can have inboard engines and be decked over.

The latter definition would also disqualify yachts from being classed as boats, but, clearly, they are not ships, despite the extraordinary size of some super yachts.

Certain smaller warships can be added to the exceptions list. Gunboats and torpedo boats from the nineteenth century and motor torpedo boats, motor gunboats and even air-sea rescue launches from the mid-twentieth century all defy the definition of a boat, but have never been classed as ships.

Historically, the definition of a ship in its strictest sense was a three-masted sailing vessel with a bowsprit and square-rigged sails on each mast. While this description is still relevant, the term now encompasses a broader spectrum of vessels.

Ships must have seagoing capability, whether
propelled by oars, sails, engine-driven paddle-
wheels, propellers, or even a combination of
these. The type of rig is now less important.

In the Age of Sail (the period between the
sixteenth and mid-nineteenth centuries),
the Royal Navy used the phrase 'His Majesty's
Ships and Vessels'. The ships referred to were
those rated from First Rate (warships with 100–
110 guns) to Sixth Rate (known as frigates and
armed with 28–32 guns). The 'vessels' were still
ships, but specifically those that were classed

CUT OF YOUR JIB

To like a person's general appearance, manner, or style. This nautical phrase related to the jib, the triangular sail set between the fore-topmast head and the jib boom. Each country had its own style of sail so a sailor could identify the nationality of the vessel from the jib.

as 'unrated' (did not have a Post Captain in command) and generally not 'ship-rigged' (had fewer than three masts).

Probably best not to bring up hovercraft, flying boats, airships or spaceships at this point...

PARTS OF
A SHIP

• • • • • • • • • • • • • • •

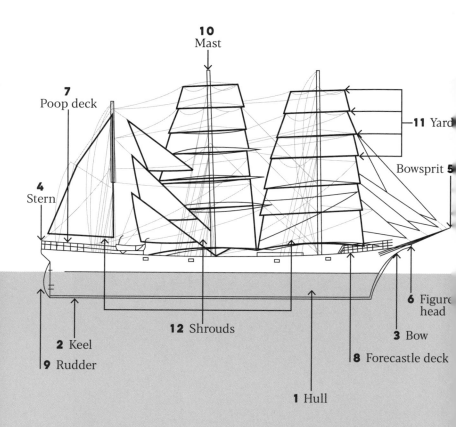

10 Mast

7 Poop deck

11 Yard

Bowspri **5**

4 Stern

6 Figure head

12 Shrouds

3 Bow

2 Keel

9 Rudder

8 Forecastle deck

1 Hull

HULL (1)

The physical structure that gives a ship its shape, size and characteristics. Everything else is attached to it or installed in it.

KEEL (2)

The long straight support that runs along the bottom of the ship's hull.

BOW (3)

The front of the ship. It can be pointed, angled, straight or flat depending on the type of vessel.

STERN (4)

The back of the ship. This can also be pointed, angled, straight or flat.

BOWSPRIT (5)

A spar (sometimes made up of more than one section) that extends over the bow. It acts as an anchor point for the lower end of the forward rigging attached to the foremast.

FIGUREHEAD (6)

A carved figure or decorative scroll at the end of the bow (stempost). The figurehead often relates to the ship-owner's family or a mythical character.

BULWARK

The built-up sides of the ship above the line of the upper deck to protect against waves and, in warships, gunfire.

UPPER DECK

The top continuous deck that stretches from bow to stern.

DECKHOUSE

The deck superstructure that accommodates the officers, crew, carpenter's workshop and galley on the upper deck.

POOP DECK (7)

The short deck at the stern of the ship, which accommodates the wheel and captain's cabins.

FORECASTLE DECK (8)

Often abbreviated to foc's'le (and pronounced *fok-sul*), this is the short deck at the front of the ship, which accommodates a windlass or capstan and provides the 'roof' for stores under the deck.

'TWEEN DECK

The deck below the upper deck (sometimes called the lower deck).

HOLD

The lowest deck of the ship, which usually contains the cargo being carried and provisions for the crew.

HATCHWAYS

The openings in the decks to allow cargo to be winched in and out of the hold.

RUDDER (9)

The blade in the water at the stern used to steer the ship.

WHEEL

Indirectly attached to the rudder and used to change the direction of the ship (it can be a tiller rather than a wheel).

MAST (10)

A wooden or metal post made in sections to varying heights and to which the rigging is attached, as well as the yards for sails. Ships can have between one and seven masts. On a ship with three or more masts, the mizzenmast is closest to the stern, the foremast is closest to the bow and the mainmast is central.

WINDLASS

A manual or electric winch for raising or lowering the anchor over the bow, or adjusting the angle of the yard arms to help the sails catch the wind.

YARDS (11)

Poles that the sails attach to and which can be rigged either across the ship or fore/aft in line with the deck.

SHROUDS (12)

The ropes or wires that go from the side of the ship up to different stations on the masts to hold them up. Ratlines (which are like rope ladders) across the shrouds give the crew a way to climb up to the yards to adjust the sails.

STERNPOST/STEMPOST

A sternpost is an upright post at the back of the boat. A stempost is a post curving up from the keel at the bow.

PARTS OF
A YACHT

. . . .

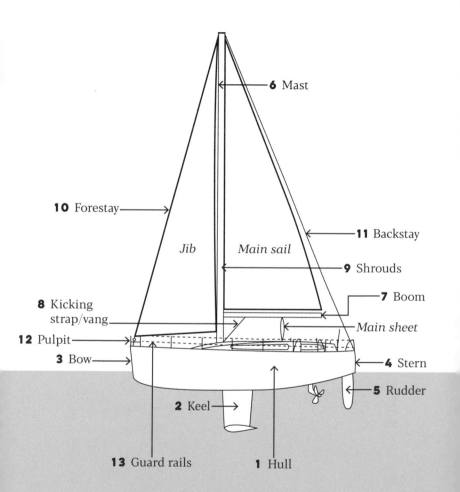

6 Mast

10 Forestay

11 Backstay

Jib

Main sail

9 Shrouds

8 Kicking
strap/vang

7 Boom

Main sheet

12 Pulpit

3 Bow

4 Stern

5 Rudder

2 Keel

13 Guard rails

1 Hull

HULL (1)

The physical structure that gives a boat its shape, size and characteristics. Everything else is attached to it or installed in it.

KEEL (2)

This can be a fin keel (a single deep-weighted blade on the underside of the boat) or a bilge keel (two or three short blades, one on the centre line and two either side). The shapes of these keels can vary depending on the design of the boat.

BOW (3)

The front of the boat. It can be pointed, angled, straight or flat depending on the type of boat.

STERN (4)

The back of the boat. This can also be pointed, angled, straight or flat.

RUDDER (5)

The blade in the water at the stern used to steer the boat.

TILLER

The beam attached to the rudder to move it (some boats have a wheel rather than a tiller).

MAST (6)

A tall post, made of wood, aluminium or carbon fibre that holds the main sail and jib or genoa up.

COCKPIT

The area where the crew work the ropes and/or from which they steer. This is usually where the entrance to below deck is.

BOOM (7)

The pole, made of wood, aluminium or carbon fibre, that holds the main sail out at the back and is attached to the mast by a gooseneck (a swivelling connection).

KICKING STRAP/VANG (8)

A rope, wire or piston system that pulls the boom downwards to create shape in the sail and stops the boom from bouncing up and down.

SHROUDS (9)

Wires that hold the mast up and help put shape into it (see forestay).

SPREADERS

Metal or wooden flattened poles attached to the mast that push the shrouds out to provide rigid strength and shape to the mast. There can be more than one set of spreaders on the mast depending on the height, type and style of rigging and mast.

FORESTAY (10)

The wire shroud attached from the top of the mast to the top of the stempost.

BACKSTAY (11)
The wire shroud attached from the top of the mast to the top of the sternpost.

HALYARDS
The ropes that hoist or drop sails, like the main sail, jib or genoa or spinnaker, or burgees and flags.

PULPIT (12)
The solid aluminium rails at the front of the boat that prevent people falling over the side.

PUSH PIT
The solid aluminium rails at the back of the boat that prevent people falling over the side.

GUARD RAILS (13)
The wires and posts along the side of the boat that prevent people falling over the side and to which fenders can also be tied.

FENDERS

Rubber or plastic inflated bladders hung over the sides or anywhere where the hull can suffer rubbing or other damage from direct contact with another surface. Often used when moored alongside a quay or another boat.

PROPELLER

Two- or more bladed object used to propel the boat along. Attached to the propeller shaft and the engine.

WINDLASS

A manual or electric winch for raising or lowering the anchor over the bow.

WINCH

The metal barrel on the deck around which ropes are passed a number of times. A winch handle in the top allows the crew to wind in the rope without having to take the pressure on the line when pulling it in.

TYPES OF SAIL

....

MAIN SAIL

The large sail at the back of the mast, attached to the boom, and overhanging the cockpit.

MAIN SHEET

The rope that controls the angle of the main sail to the centre of the boat. It is attached at the top to the boom through a series of pulley blocks and at the bottom on a block attached to a slide known as a running horse.

JIB

The sails at the front of the mast, usually attached at deck level near the bow to a point at least two-thirds of the way up the mast.

JIB SHEETS

Ropes that can be pulled in or let out to control the shape and angle of the jib or genoa.

GENOA

See jib. The genoa (or genny) is larger than the jib and overlaps the main sail.

SPINNAKER

An often colourful sail used at the front of the boat to give downwind speed. It is also called a 'conventional' or 'symmetric' spinnaker. It can be used with the wind directly behind the boat's stern.

SPINNAKER SHEETS

The ropes used to control the shape of the spinnaker (and gennaker) by pulling them in or letting them out.

GENNAKER

Also known as an 'asymmetric' spinnaker. It is a cross between the genoa and spinnaker and used for sailing downwind. Unlike the conventional spinnaker, it cannot be used with the

wind directly behind the boat's stern, but is sailed at an angle to the wind to give speed.

REEFING LINES

Ropes that run along the inside of the boom to each end of the sail. When pulled upon they gather the sail up from the bottom, making the sail area smaller in stronger winds. There can be more than one reefing point on a sail so that the sail can be made smaller gradually.

ICONIC
VESSELS
· · · · · · · · · · · · · · · · · · ·

THE ANGLO-SAXON SHIP AT SUTTON HOO

The discovery of this ship full of extraordinary treasures in East Anglia in 1939 completely changed our understanding of Anglo-Saxon craftsmanship and sophistication. Thought to be the AD *c*.624 burial site of King Rædwald of East Anglia, the finding cast the 'Dark Ages' in an entirely new light.

THE *MARY ROSE*

King Henry VIII's favourite vessel was launched in 1511. It featured innovative gunports for heavy guns. Having served in several campaigns, it was refitted in 1536 to carry even more guns. The ship sank during the Battle of the Solent in 1545 with the loss of around 500 lives. Raised in 1982, it's now a Tudor time-capsule at its permanent site in Portsmouth.

THE *MAYFLOWER*

In 1620, around 130 passengers and crew left England for the 'New World' on board the *Mayflower* in search of religious freedom. Terrible weather forced the Pilgrims, as they became known, to settle in Massachusetts, further north than agreed. To quell disagreements, they created the Mayflower Compact, considered to be a seed of American democracy.

HM BARK *ENDEAVOUR*

Endeavour was the first European ship to reach the east coast of Australia in 1770, setting out for the Pacific Ocean in 1768. Officially, Lieutenant James Cook's research vessel was to observe the transit of Venus. But sealed orders from the Admiralty also instructed that he take possession of the southern continent. He charted the coast of New Zealand and proclaimed British sovereignty over the territories and the Indigenous populations who already lived there.

WIDE BERTH

More widely used today to mean keeping an adequate distance from a person or object, this maritime term comes from ships also keeping sufficient distance between them to avoid causing each other damage when berthed.

HMS *VICTORY*

Launched in 1765, *Victory* was the largest ship of its day. The wood from more than 2,000 oak trees was used to build the hull. In 1803 it became Admiral Horatio Nelson's flagship and was the site of his death during the Battle of Trafalgar in 1805. Today, the ship is the oldest still commissioned in naval service.

CUTTY SARK

Built in 1869 for the China tea trade, *Cutty Sark* was the pinnacle of clipper-ship design and one of the fastest vessels of its time. After a lengthy career, it was preserved in Greenwich as the very last of its kind – a tribute to the glorious days of sail and memorial to the Merchant Navy.

HMT *EMPIRE WINDRUSH*

In June 1948, *Empire Windrush* arrived in the UK from Jamaica carrying more than 1,000 passengers in search of a new life. It wasn't the first ship to bring migrants from the Caribbean to Britain but it has since become symbolic of the arrival of a generation of migrants from the Commonwealth, who came to help rebuild post-war Britain and make it their home.

FIVE EXPLORERS WHO CHANGED THE WORLD

....

As well as achievements in art and science, the Renaissance ushered in a golden age of European maritime exploration. But our concept of the great European explorers is rather romanticised. We like to think of them as great agents of progress, choosing to set their courses into uncharted waters when some people still believed the world was flat. However, the truth is that Ferdinand Magellan and his contemporaries weren't necessarily motivated by a simple desire to explore.

HENRY THE NAVIGATOR (1394–1460)

Before Prince Henry of Portugal ('Henry the Navigator') and Vasco da Gama helped turn Portugal into an imperial power and one of the wealthiest countries fifteenth- and sixteenth-century Europe, long-distance maritime exploration and trade was considered a dangerous and unreliable sideline. Even prior to Marco Polo's thirteenth-century travels,

journeys to the East relied on overland routes along the Silk Road.

MARCO POLO

After Henry helped develop the caravel – a lighter, faster, more manoeuvrable ship better suited to long voyages into uncharted waters – it was da Gama who first linked Europe and Asia by sea. His 1497–99 expedition was the longest ever recorded by the time he returned and made even longer by having to avoid flashpoints in the Mediterranean and around the Arabian peninsula. The route was, however, still quicker than travelling the Silk Road.

VASCO DA GAMA (1460–1524)

Da Gama's voyage around the Cape of Good Hope to India took place between 1497–99. The charts he returned with gave Portugal dominance over the spice trade, which is precisely why he had been given the commission in the first place. His Portuguese sponsors fully expected to buy more in the East than they would sell, so where the money went, soldiers soon followed to protect it. The age of European imperial expansion into the East had begun.

FERDINAND MAGELLAN (1480–1521)

Magellan's attempted circumnavigation of

the globe was something of a response to what da Gama had achieved 20 years before. With Portugal now dominating the eastward route, the race was on amongst other European countries to find an alternative, westward route.

Magellan set sail from Spain in 1519, fully expecting the westward route to be shorter. Amerigo Vespucci and Christopher Columbus had already established that there was another continent between western Europe and the East, but after Magellan found a sea route through it (he was not the one to name it the Strait of Magellan himself) he fully expected

AMERIGO VESPUCCI

CHRISTOPHER COLUMBUS

to find Asia another few days' sail beyond the western coast of the Americas. Instead he had to sail for almost another four months before finding land again. He had inadvertently sailed across an entire ocean. Finding it pleasantly calm compared to the tempestuous seas around the southern tip of the Americas, he named it Pacifico.

But Magellan did not actually complete the circumnavigation for which he is famous. He was killed in the Philippines in 1521, only three quarters of the way around the globe, as the crow flies. The circumnavigation was completed by the sole surviving ship of the five he had set out with, manned by fewer than 20 of the original 270 men.

FRANCIS DRAKE (C.1540-96)

After Magellan, Spain continued to look to the west rather than the east, building up a sizeable empire in the Americas. It was here they

encountered the scourge of the Spanish Main, someone they issued with bounties equivalent to millions in today's bullion, but who became something of an English folk hero because of his escapades – Sir Francis Drake. He's a controversial figure these days, even in the context of the times, given that he only became a privateer, attacking Spanish towns and ships in their colonies, after a career trading enslaved people.

In 1577, Drake set off to disrupt Spanish trade, to chart the west coast of the Americas and to find a better route around the globe than the one Magellan's crew had charted, although he ultimately followed a similar track. Even when their companion ships and crews were lost, Drake and the crew of the *Golden Hind* continued to plunder many of the Spanish towns and ships they came across. When they returned to England in 1580, the crown's half-share of the treasure made up the majority of Elizabeth I's income that year.

FRANCIS DRAKE

JAMES COOK (1728-79)

The die had been cast as far as the unsus-pecting peoples of the non-European world were concerned. The explorers who weren't invaders brought back maps for those who followed. Two centuries after Drake's circum-navigation, James Cook was sent in search of a fabled southern continent and to explore the Pacific and polar regions, and in doing so charted thousands of miles that had never been mapped before – a cartographic legacy that sur-vives to this day.

It is not hard to imagine what the people who had been living in the area Cook promptly renamed New South Wales for tens of thou-sands of years before he 'discovered' it thought. For them, and probably many of the other peo-ples and countries happened across by these European explorers, that Enlightenment spirit of progress must have seemed more than a little one-sided.

FIVE
INCREDIBLE
VOYAGES

. . . .

THE SEARCH FOR THE NORTHWEST PASSAGE

In 1906, three years after they set sail, Norwegian explorer Roald Amundsen and his five-man crew became the first people to cross from the Atlantic to the Pacific through the waters of the Canadian passage – successfully navigating the treacherous Northwest Passage. While Amundsen and his men were the first to achieve this feat by boat alone, they were not the first to traverse the Passage; Robert McClure, an Irishman, had made the same journey west-to-east by ship, sledge and ship again more than 50 years earlier in 1850–54.

DEAD IN THE WATER
Whether referring to a career or a project this phrase means to have no momentum or chance of progression. Its maritime origins referred to a ship that is motionless, usually on a windless day.

Today Amundsen is perhaps more famous for being the first man to reach the South Pole five years later, but at the time both achievements brought him widespread acclaim.

Amundsen's success story might almost seem prosaic compared to the legend that built up around the unforgiving waters of the North-west Passage over many centuries. Numerous expeditions were sent to investigate an open water route that would facilitate trade between Europe and Asia but many turned back, finding their way blocked by ice and conditions for which they could not have prepared.

THE LOSS OF *EREBUS* AND *TERROR*

The most famous expedition to search for the Northwest Passage set out in 1845 under the command of Sir John Franklin. The two ships, *Erebus* and *Terror*, had previously undertaken successful voyages in difficult polar conditions and proven to be exceptionally resilient. Loaded with enough provisions and hunting equipment to last three years, and crewed by experienced officers, the ships were expected to overwinter in moving ice fields before continuing their journey north as the ice thawed each spring. In fact, having been icebound for more than a year, the vessels were abandoned in April 1848, by which time Franklin and 15 of his men had already perished. In total, more than 30 expeditions were sent out to discover the fate of *Erebus* and *Terror*, of which Robert McClure's was one, and the wrecks were finally located, with the assistance of Inuit communities, in 2014 and 2016 respectively.

MUTINY ON THE *BOUNTY*

Many of the most famous voyages in history are notable precisely because things didn't go to plan. William Bligh would have been a brief footnote in history had events on HMS *Bounty's* expedition to transport breadfruit from Tahiti to British colonies in the West Indies in 1789 transpired differently. Instead, he has become infamous or a misunderstood hero, depending on whose version of the story is to be believed.

After five months on Tahiti, spent enjoying their idyllic surrounds and the companionship of the local communities, many of the

Bounty's crew were unhappy about leaving and the return to shipboard discipline. Once at sea, a rebellion led by master's mate Fletcher Christian, thought to have been singled out by Bligh for rule-breaking, resulted in the captain being taken prisoner on board his own vessel. Nearly half the crew remained loyal to him and were allowed by Christian's mutineers to leave the ship in a 23 ft (7 m) open boat. Nobody, on either side, seriously expected 19 people to survive with less than five days' worth of supplies, 1,300 miles (2,100 km) away from Tahiti.

In truth, Bligh managed to save all but one of his supporters, sailing an astonishing 4,000 miles (6,500 km) to safety in Timor, raising morale by singing songs as storms threatened to overturn the dangerously overloaded boat for significant stretches of the journey. It took a long time for Bligh's reputation to recover from the demolition of his character perpetrated by Fletcher Christian's lawyer brother to justify what had happened, but that open-boat journey a sixth of the way around the globe remains one of the greatest feats of sailing in history.

CHARLES DARWIN AND THE *BEAGLE*

Charles Darwin almost didn't join Captain Robert FitzRoy in 1831 for the second survey mission of HMS *Beagle*, but FitzRoy, himself a scientist, wanted a geologist and naturalist on board and the 22-year-old Darwin, recently graduated from Cambridge, seemed a good fit.

PLAIN SAILING
This literally means easy-going and unobstructed progress. The maritime saying comes from when sailors found the sailing easy and uncomplicated.

What was intended as a two-year expedition stretched to five, carrying out surveys of South America before returning to Britain via Australia, completing a circumnavigation in the process. As a 'gentleman naturalist' Darwin would leave the ship for weeks at a time. His log of the voyage built his reputation 20 years before *On the Origin of Species*. Instead of following his original plan to become a parson on his return, Darwin set to answering some of the greatest scientific questions of the time.

ERNEST SHACKLETON AND THE *ENDURANCE*

Ernest Shackleton may not have made his name as perhaps the last great explorer of Antarctica had his most famous expedition been as successful as that of Roald Amundsen. He is renowned for the extraordinary feat he achieved in managing to turn life-threatening misfortune into a heroic act of salvation and survival.

A member of Robert Falcon Scott's crew on the *Discovery* expedition to explore Antarctica in 1901–03, Shackleton set higher ambitions for his own voyage of 1914–17. His ship, the *Endurance*, was to drop him at the edge of the ice shelf in the Weddell Sea, as close to the South Pole as possible, and he would then complete the first continental crossing by dog sledge. In the end the *Endurance* didn't even get close to the Pole, becoming trapped in pack ice in February 1915. Shackleton planned to wait until

the ice melted and released the ship in the spring before continuing, but the *Endurance* was slowly crushed and ultimately sank in November 1915.

The crew spent the Antarctic summer camped on the icefloe in tents, having salvaged food from the wrecked ship and surviving on seal

meat. In April 1916 they set sail in three life-boats for the nearest land. They arrived five days later on the remote Elephant Island. From here, Shackleton took a lifeboat and five men and sailed a further 800 miles (1,300 km) to South Georgia to summon help. Climbing a mountain range to reach a Norwegian whaling station, Shackleton made four attempts to rescue the men he had left on Elephant Island.

TO THE BITTER END
The bitter end is the part of an anchor chain that remains on board when the ship is at anchor. To reach the bitter end now means to go as far as you can go.

It was the Chilean tug *Yelcho* that succeeded and, in August 1916, all 22 men he had left some four and a half months previously were finally able to return home.

THE OCEANS
OF THE WORLD
IN NUMBERS

. . . .

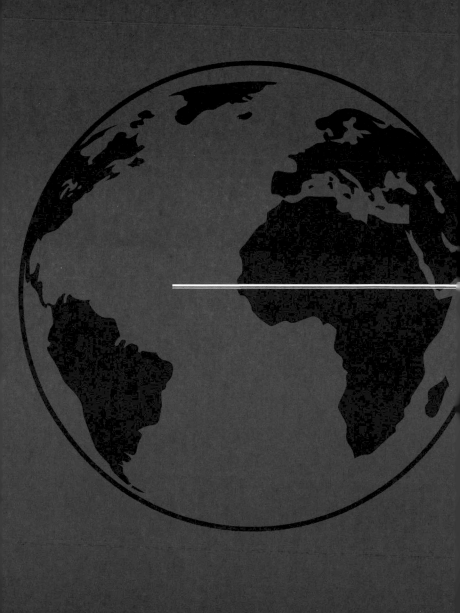

30%

30%

The proportion of Earth's surface covered by the world's largest ocean, the Pacific – at 63 million square miles, (163 million square km) it contains half of all free water on the planet.

5 MOONS

At the widest point, from Colombia to Indonesia, the Pacific is 12,300 miles (19,800 km) across – 5 times the diameter of the Moon.

1,670 MILES

The furthest point from land anywhere on the planet is Point Nemo, named after the character in Jules Verne's *Twenty Thousand Leagues Under the Sea.*

1,000 YEARS

All the oceans are just one big body of water – but it would take a single drop of water a millennium to traverse all of it.

12,100 FEET

The average depth of
the ocean (3,688 m or
2.3 miles) the world's
current tallest building,
Burj Khalifa, is 2,723 ft
(830 m).

35,876 FEET

The deepest part of the
ocean is the Challenger
Deep (named after
the Royal Navy ship
that first recorded its
depth in the 1870s)
in the Mariana Trench
(10,935 m or 6.8 miles) –
Mount Everest is 29,377
ft (8,848 m).

50 AIRLINERS

The pressure in the Challenger Deep is 15,750 pounds per square inch, 1,071 times the pressure at sea level – equivalent to 50 commercial jets crushing down on top of you.

1,090 FEET

The deepest scuba dive in history (332 m) – it took 15 minutes to descend and over 13 hours to get back up to avoid decompression sickness.

```
0                    1
INCH
```

1 INCH

The oceans contain 321 million cubic miles of water, out of 332.5 million on the entire planet – all of the water in the atmosphere could fit in the top 1 inch of the ocean.

230 FEET

Only about 2% of the water on the planet is frozen (mostly in the polar regions), but if it all melted at the same time the sea level would rise by 70 m (230 ft) – almost enough to cover New York's Statue of Liberty.

40,390 MILES

The largest mountain range on Earth, the Mid-Ocean Ridge (65,000 km), is actually underwater – the circumference of the planet is only 25,000 miles (40,000 km).

90%

The percentage of Earth's volcanic activity that happens in the oceans.

1,700 FEET

The largest tsunami
ever recorded flooded
Lituya Bay, Alaska,
in 1958 after a landslide
of 90 million tons
of rock fell into the
narrow bay.

94%

The oceans are home
to most of the life on
Earth.

THE MOST AMAZING SEA CREATURES

....

BLOBFISH

With few muscles to help it swim, and reliant on the currents to carry its buoyant jelly body close to food, the blobfish perhaps has good reason to resemble a sad face.

FANGTOOTH

Proportionate to the size of its body, the fang-tooth's teeth are the largest of any sea creature – they're so long that when its mouth is closed, the teeth have to fit into specialised spaces on either side of its brain.

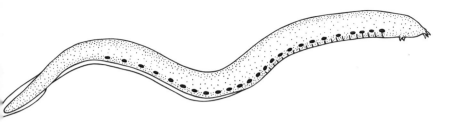

HAGFISH

Also known as the slime eel, the hagfish not only secretes sticky mucus, but it can tie itself in a knot to squeeze out more, making it too slippery to seize and choking the gills of would-be predators.

TONGUE-EATING LOUSE

Looking like a 1.5 in (3.8 cm) underwater woodlouse, the delightfully named tongue-eating louse enters a red snapper's gills, eats its tongue and then sits in its mouth enjoying whatever the host consumes.

PHRONIMA

Like something out of a science fiction horror movie, the transparent shrimp-like phronima burrows inside a salp, hollows it out, lays its eggs, then rides around in the dead salp like a submarine.

SEA CUCUMBER

Some pearl fish and pea crabs can live in a sea cucumber's digestive system. Predators can look forward to the sea cucumber ejecting part of their gut (which they can then regenerate) to fend them off with its toxic insides.

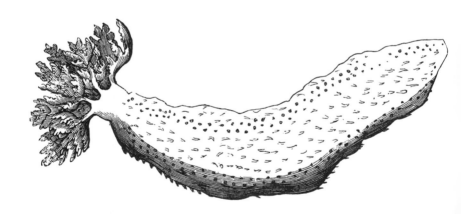

SEA STAR

It's widely known that many species of sea stars can lose an arm and grow into another, but in some species the lost arm can grow another sea star entirely.

PORTUGUESE MAN OF WAR

The Portuguese man of war is actually a colony of four symbiotic creatures: one buoyant polyp; one made of tentacles; one for eating and digesting; and one for reproducing.

TAKE THE WIND OUT OF HIS SAILS

To take the wind out of someone's sails means to drain their enthusiasm or initiative. This is derived from when a vessel could slow another one down by getting between it and the wind, preventing their sails from filling.

AMERICAN ANGLERFISH

Sold as monkfish in shops, and also known as the all-mouth, the American anglerfish has such a huge mouth that some come to the surface and swallow seabirds whole. Other species of anglerfish have light-up lures to draw prey in.

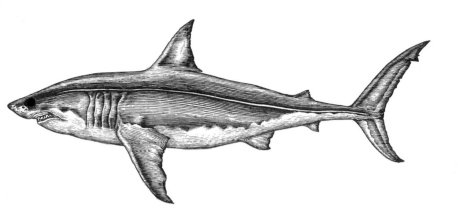

GREAT WHITE SHARK

The ultimate predator, growing up to 21 ft
(6.4 m), weighing 5,000 lb (2,300 kg) and swimming at speeds as great as 35 mph (56.3 kph),
the great white shark has the largest teeth of
any shark at up to 3 in (7.5 cm), with the same
force behind them as a truck resting on top of
a knife.

EIGHT FAMOUS
SEA BATTLES

. . . .

THE SPANISH ARMADA (1588)

The Armada Campaign, from July to August 1588, was a defining moment in English history. It stemmed from the desire of King Philip II of Spain to satisfy his dynastic ambitions and religious obligations, both of which involved invading England. Fortunately for Queen Elizabeth I (whose famous speech rallying the troops at Tilbury that August later added to the legendary status of the victory), her large but badly organised and hastily assembled English fleet prevented the slightly smaller and better-organised Spanish fleet from conducting

> *I know I have the body of a weak and feeble woman; but I have the heart and stomach of a king, and of a king of England too, and think foul scorn that Parma or Spain, or any prince of Europe, should dare to invade the borders of my realm...*
>
> **– Queen Elizabeth I, 9 August 1588**

its poorly thought-out invasion plan. Dutch naval intervention meant the Spanish might well have failed even if the English fleet had not bothered to turn up. The campaign was a demonstration of the impossibility of coordinated strategic manoeuvres with sixteenth century communications.

THE BATTLE OF TRAFALGAR (1805)

By the first decade of the nineteenth century, Europe was dominated by Napoleon Bonaparte. Outstandingly successful on land, Napoleon and his navy were never able to overcome Britain at sea. Perhaps the most famous – if not the most decisive – naval battle of the Napoleonic Wars was the Battle of Trafalgar, fought on 21 October 1805. In a by-then familiar pattern, a well-drilled, cohesive and experienced British fleet under Horatio Nelson defeated a comparatively demoralised and poorly trained Franco-Spanish force in a lopsided victory that

was foreseen even by the French admiral, Ville-neuve. In the short term, Britain reduced the threat of a French invasion from non-existent to even more non-existent. In the longer term, the nation gained an enduring legend in the form of the slain Nelson.

THE BATTLE OF THE IRONCLADS (1862)

Little happened in the immediate aftermath of the Napoleonic Wars to challenge British naval supremacy, but 50 years later advances in propulsion, guns and armour presented new threats. The American Civil War broke out in 1861 and within months saw the first battle between iron-armoured warships. On 8 March 1862 the Confederate ironclad CSS *Virginia* created a panic by single-handedly sinking two powerfully armed but wooden-hulled Union warships and damaging a third. The next day it

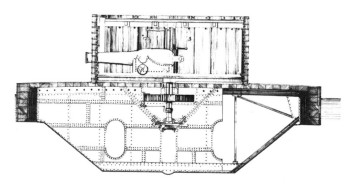

encountered the Union ironclad USS *Monitor* and an epic confrontation began between the two unwieldy opponents (*Virginia* required nearly 30 minutes to execute a 180° turn). After hours of fruitlessly bouncing shot and shell off each other's armoured sides both combatants retired to claim victory. The battle was tactically a draw, but it signalled the dawn of a new era in naval warfare.

THE BATTLE OF TSUSHIMA (1905)

The latter half of the nineteenth century saw few significant naval engagements, and while the battles of Lissa (1866) and the Yalu (1894) gave some sense of the future of naval warfare, it was not until the Russo-Japanese War of 1904–05 that a battle occurred that caught the attention of naval experts the world over. The Battle of Tsushima, fought on 27 May 1905, is still seen as the defining naval action of this war. After an epic, wearing voyage around the world, the Russian Baltic Fleet (rebranded for the occasion as the Second Pacific Squadron) was intercepted and annihilated off the Tsushima Straits by the Imperial Japanese Navy.

In practical terms, a Russian victory was unlikely. Many of their vessels were in dire need of maintenance. Their ships were an unbalanced collection ranging from then-modern battleships hampered by poor construction to museum pieces that should never have been sent. To make matters worse, the morale of the Russian crews, from stokers to admiral, was low. By contrast, the Japanese fleet was fresh, having had an opportunity to refit its ships and train its crews after the battles of 1904, and at Tsushima was at the peak of efficiency. These factors were largely invisible to outside observers, and the comprehensive defeat of an established European power came as a shock to many.

THE BATTLE OF JUTLAND (1916)

The apparent lesson of Tsushima was that the 'big gun' battleship was the ultimate arbiter of naval warfare. The Great Powers continued to build more and the naval arms race intensified when Britain unveiled HMS *Dreadnought* in 1906. By 1914, the leading players in the naval arms race were Britain and Germany, and when the First World War broke out everyone expected a gigantic clash between their respective fleets. Eventually, the Battle of Jutland took place from 31 May to 1 June 1916. It remains the largest naval battle ever fought between 'big gun' battleships and the only such action to occur during the First World War.

After months of waiting, virtually the full might of the British Grand Fleet and the German High Seas Fleet clashed in the North Sea. To palpable disappointment in Britain the battle was inconclusive, and, while losses were heavy on both sides, the balance of human and material casualties significantly favoured the Germans. However, the German aim of breaking the British maritime blockade failed, forcing them to consider shifting their strategic emphasis to the ultimately more effective use of submarine warfare. A demonstration of huge expenditure of life and material for little tangible tactical benefit, Jutland sits alongside many other major battles of the First World War in popular perception.

THE BATTLE OF MIDWAY (1942)

While battleships were living out the last of their useful years of service, the Second World War saw the rise of a powerful, new ship in the form of the aircraft carrier, which convincingly ousted 'big gun' ships from their pedestal. The most famous aircraft carrier battle in history is the Battle of Midway, which took place on 4 June 1942. As part of an ill-considered plan to seize Midway Island in the Central Pacific, the Japanese despatched their premier carrier strike force, the Dai Ichi Kido Butai. Aided by signals intelligence, the US Navy ambushed the four Japanese aircraft carriers with three of their own. The Japanese demonstrated somewhat better aircraft-handling overall, but the battle cruelly exposed the inadequacies of their anti-aircraft defences and damage control arrangements. The exchange of blows by both sides' aircraft saw all four Japanese carriers sunk but the loss of only one US carrier. Although the now weakened Imperial

Japanese Navy went on to inflict future defeats on Allied forces, the ships and strategic initiative lost at Midway proved irreplaceable.

THE BATTLE OF THE NORTH CAPE (1943)

The last 'big gun' action in European waters was the Battle of the North Cape, fought on 26 December 1943. In a poorly conceived operation intended to prove to Hitler that the German surface fleet was not obsolete, the battlecruiser *Scharnhorst* was despatched from its Norwegian base to intercept and destroy convoy JW55B en route to north Russia. In atrocious weather, the *Scharnhorst's* initial attack was prevented by a trio of weaker British cruisers. In the ensuing confusion, one of these ships – HMS *Belfast* – found itself in the unenviable position of pursuing *Scharnhorst* alone. While attempting to disengage, *Scharnhorst* was finally sunk, falling victim to the guns of the battleship HMS *Duke of York*

and the torpedoes of its escorts. In the wake of *Scharnhorst's* loss, Hitler forbade further offensive operations by 'useless' battleships and battlecruisers.

THE FALKLANDS WAR (1982)

In the aftermath of the Second World War, naval technology continued to evolve at a frightening rate, with jet aircraft, missiles and nuclear submarines all making their mark in the Cold War era. Perhaps fortunately, this period saw no major war between the main powers of the day. The only exception was the Falkland Islands campaign between 2 April and 14 June 1982. Argentinian military forces seized the Falklands Islands in what their leaders assumed would be an uncontested occupation of a strategic territory. The British responded by despatching a task force to retake the Falklands, resulting in a prolonged and difficult campaign where the slight technological edge enjoyed by the Royal Navy was offset by extremely challenging logistical issues. The fighting at sea became a proving ground for untried naval weapon systems, punctuated by the occasional use of 1940s technology (including the torpedo that sank the Argentinian cruiser *General Belgrano*, itself of pre-Second World War vintage). After heavy losses on both sides, the British ultimately prevailed.

TEN DEADLY
DISASTERS
AT SEA

·················

TEK SING (1822)

For most of human history travel by sea has been inherently risky, but some of the worst maritime disasters have almost been forgotten. In 1822, more than 2,000 people squeezed on to the junk *Tek Sing*, on its way from China to Java and the sugar cane fields of Indonesia. With fresh water supplies dwindling, and hoping to escape a monsoon, the captain took a shortcut around the wrong side of an island, despite knowing it was risky in rough seas. It was impossible to tell the difference between wind-swept water and water breaking over shoals. The *Tek Sing* hit a reef and the wooden vessel immediately began to break apart. Strong winds and the tide pulled it over as it sank. There were only a few hundred survivors. At least 1,600 people died – more than on the *Titanic* almost a century later.

RMS *TITANIC* (1912)

The consequences of negligence, lack of skills and poor communication can be fatal. But other factors that are beyond the sailor's control have also contributed to disasters at sea. Research shows that a series of warm years in the Arctic before 1912 caused more icebergs to break off the coast of Greenland and drift further south than usual, right into the path of the *Titanic*. The collision led to the loss of more than 1,500 people, compounded by the insufficient number of lifeboats. Though not the most deadly maritime disaster in modern history, it is undoubtedly the most famous, probably because so many considered the *Titanic* unsinkable. The sinking led to regulations being put in place that all ships must have sufficient lifeboats for everyone on board.

HMS *ABOUKIR*, *HOGUE* AND *CRESSY* (1914)

In the early twentieth century, during wartime, vessels had to deal with a new unseen enemy: the submarine. While successful countermeasures were later developed, submarines proved to be the bane of many ships. The Royal Navy cruisers *Aboukir*, *Hogue* and *Cressy* were all sunk within an hour by a German submarine on 22 September 1914. The captain of the *Cressy* was faced with a moral dilemma. *Aboukir* and *Hogue* had already been sunk and he had to decide whether to leave the stricken vessels and save his own ship, or stay behind and rescue his comrades. He chose the latter option, but consequently the *Cressy* was also sunk by the submarine. This is a fine example of the moral duty sailors feel they have to rescue fellow seamen in mortal danger, although at the time the Navy viewed the captain's decision less kindly.

RMS *LUSITANIA* (1915)

One of the most famous sinkings by submarine was that of the ocean liner *Lusitania*, on 7 May 1915. The Admiralty had already issued warnings of submarine activity when the ship was sighted and torpedoed by a German submarine. The absence of nearby rescue vessels and the rapidity of its demise led to the loss of nearly 1,200 lives, more than a tenth of them American. The event has been seen as a possible trigger for the United States to eventually enter the First World War in 1917, as the tide of public opinion began to turn against Germany.

THE HALIFAX EXPLOSION (1917)

Effective communication at sea is an essential skill and a lack of good communication between ships has been a cause of numerous disasters at sea, the most devastating of which was the 1917 Halifax Explosion. In the port of Halifax, Nova Scotia, the master of the Norwegian vessel *Imo* refused to cede right of way to

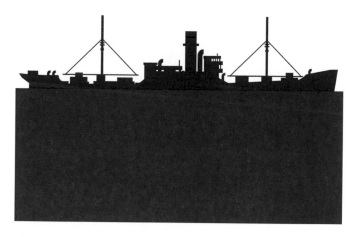

the *Mont Blanc*, a French ammunition ship heavily loaded with explosives. The resulting collision started a fire on board *Mont Blanc*, eventually causing it to explode. The explosion was so fierce it momentarily exposed the harbour floor beneath it, destroyed over 400 acres of surrounding land and killed approximately 2,000 people. With the exception of the atomic bombs on Hiroshima and Nagasaki in 1945, it was the largest manmade explosion of all time.

RMS *LANCASTRIA* (1940)

Britain's worst maritime disaster has largely been forgotten. In 1940, hundreds of thousands of British troops remained stuck in France after the evacuation of Dunkirk and headed along the coast to St Nazaire, where ships such as the *Lancastria* were waiting. The grand liner had been used as a troop transport since the start of the Second World War and its captain had orders to overlook legal limits on passenger numbers and evacuate as many people as possible. The crew stopped counting at 6,000 and many more boarded after that. As the *Lancastria* left France, German planes dive-bombed, scoring three direct hits. The ship sank in barely 20 minutes, with only time to launch two lifeboats. At least 4,000 people were still stuck inside – some estimates suggest up to 6,000 may have died. Back in Britain, how-ever, the news was suppressed for fear it would break morale. By the time it became more widely known, it was as one of many similarly large tragedies experienced during the Second World War.

WILHELM GUSTLOFF (1945)

The worst wartime maritime disaster in history has also been mostly forgotten. The ocean liner *Wilhelm Gustloff* was carrying German families across the Baltic away from the approaching Soviet army in January 1945 when it was hit by three Soviet torpedoes. About 10,800 people were on board. The ship was so full that several hundred people were sitting in a drained swimming pool. It sank in under an hour and, despite being barely 20 miles from the coast, escape was not possible – thousands of people were stuck inside, lifeboats were frozen to their davits and air temperatures were well below zero. Just as happened after the *Titanic* sank, even those who survived the sinking couldn't last long in the freezing water. Up to 10,000 people on board the *Wilhelm Gustloff* may have died, thousands of them children, but the Nazi regime suppressed the news.

USS *INDIANAPOLIS* (1945)

We often consider the immediate death toll when a maritime disaster strikes, but there have been many cases where the majority of fatalities occur afterwards, as a direct consequence of the incident. The sinking of the American cruiser *Indianapolis*, made famous

by Robert Shaw's monologue in the film *Jaws*, is one example. The ship was hit by a Japanese submarine and sank rapidly, but most of the deaths were caused by dehydration, hypo-thermia and shark attacks. Only around 310 of a crew of nearly 1,200 survived the disaster. The saddest part of this tragic event was that more lives could have been saved had the US Navy reacted faster in its rescue effort.

HERALD OF FREE ENTERPRISE (1987)

One of the most harrowing aspects of maritime disasters is how quickly things can go wrong and through such small human error. The sinking of the roll on/roll off ferry *Herald of Free Enterprise* in March 1987 is one such example. When the ferry departed from Zebrugge, the bow door was accidently left open, allowing the sea water to pour into the decks. Within minutes, less than one mile from the port, the ship capsized onto its side and 193 lives were lost. Human error (the crewman responsible for checking the bow door was shut was asleep in his cabin at the time), vessel design flaws (it had no watertight compartments) and negligence from the shipping company were seen as the primary causes of the disaster and improvements were soon made to subsequent ships.

TURN A BLIND EYE

To refuse to acknowledge something that you know to be occurring. During the Battle of Copenhagen in 1801, Vice-Admiral Nelson led the British attack against the anchored joint Danish/Norwegian fleet. Above Nelson, the British fleet was commanded by Admiral Sir Hyde Parker. The two men disagreed over tactics and at one point Hyde Parker sent a signal (by the use of flags) instructing Nelson to disengage. Nelson was convinced he could win if he persisted and that's when he held his spyglass to his blind eye and insisted he didn't see the signal. In their biography, The Life of Admiral Lord Nelson, *published just eight years later, Clarke and M'Arthur printed what they claimed to be Nelson's actual words at the time: 'You know, Foley, I have only one eye – and I have a right to be blind sometimes... I really do not see the signal.'*

DOÑA PAZ (1987)

Despite all the regulations that have been brought in, when they are ignored, there is still scope for almost inconceivable tragedy. In the worst peacetime maritime disaster in history, the passenger ferry *Doña Paz* had capacity for a maximum of 1,500 people, but, shortly before Christmas 1987, it was carrying almost 4,500 between Tacloban and Manila in the Philippines. Allegedly sailing without a radio, it collided with the oil tanker *Vector* (which didn't have a lookout on duty) at 10.30 p.m. The power immediately went out, meaning the thousands of people overcrowding the lower decks didn't stand a chance. Oil spilling from the *Vector* quickly caught alight, which meant the *Doña Paz*'s unsuitable wooden lifeboats couldn't be launched, and it was too far for anyone jumping from the ferry's top deck to swim under the flames. Though the ferry stayed afloat for two hours, there were only 24 survivors.

ELEVEN
NOTORIOUS
PIRATES

. . . .

FRANÇOIS L'OLONNAIS (1630-69)

His reputation may have been eclipsed by pirates who came later, but French buccaneer l'Olonnais was perhaps the most brutal of the lot. With a particular hatred of Spain, he terrorised the Spanish Main, attacking settlements from the sea, killing most of the people he found so that the survivors would give him information, such as the movements of the Spanish navy. He was infamous for torturing his victims, burning them, cutting out their tongues, removing their eyes and, allegedly, he once cut out a man's heart and took a bite of it to persuade the rest of the crew to give him what he wanted.

HENRY MORGAN (1635-88)

Not as brutal in his methods as l'Olonnais, shrewd Welsh pirate Morgan also focused on Spanish settlements and avoided attacking any British targets so that the Royal Navy would turn a blind eye. Unfortunately, news of a peace treaty between Britain and Spain was slow to reach the Caribbean, so Morgan sacked the Spanish colony of Panama and the British were forced to arrest him and take him back to England. But there he was feted as a hero, the true heir to Francis Drake. He was duly knighted and sent to Jamaica as its deputy governor. Who better to protect the colony in case the Spanish attacked?

WILLIAM KIDD (1645-1701)

Some historians aren't convinced Captain Kidd should even be considered a pirate. Employed by the British government as a privateer (effectively a mercenary with authority to attack enemy shipping), he was even commissioned to hunt pirates at one point. After capturing a ship filled with gold and silver from India in 1698, he learnt he had been branded a pirate and headed to the American colonies to protest his innocence. Instead, he was hanged for murder and piracy, and gibbeted in Tilbury Docks. Legend has it that most of his treasure is still hidden somewhere in the Caribbean.

BENJAMIN HORNIGOLD (1680-1719)

A successful privateer who turned to piracy, Hornigold was something of the godfather of pirates. Not only did he mentor Blackbeard, Black Sam and Stede Bonnet, he was also one of the leaders of the Republic of Pirates, which established a pirate code between 1706 and 1718, giving crews democratic votes on who should be captain and requiring all pirates to treat each other civilly – regardless of how they treated their victims. The Republic only disbanded after the King of England offered

pardons to pirates, which Hornigold himself took and subsequently became a pirate hunter looking for many of his old comrades.

BLACKBEARD (C.1680–1718)

Hornigold's former second-in-command Edward Teach now embodies our classic image of a pirate – which is exactly how Teach would have liked it. He boarded ships in a cloud of smoke, with lit fuses tucked under his hat and tied into the pigtails of his great black beard and with copious guns and knives strapped to his chest. It was all part of an attempt to generate a

fearsome reputation so that his targets would surrender without a fight. Blackbeard wasn't actually that successful as a pirate, he never amassed a great fortune, and was killed in an ambush after attempting to secure a pardon.

STEDE BONNET (1688–1718)

Bonnet is sometimes considered the worst pirate of all time – but not because of anything he did. While most pirates were common criminals or poor sailors who had deserted, Bonnet was called the Gentleman Pirate because he was a respected member of Barbadian society, the heir to a sugar plantation, who got carried away by fantasies of an adventurous life at sea. So, he bought a ship and hired a crew, despite not knowing anything about being a pirate or, indeed, sailing. He blundered, rather than plundered, his way around the Caribbean, at one point sailing with Blackbeard until Blackbeard realised he was a complete amateur, took him prisoner and then abandoned him.

BLACK SAM (1689–1717)

Samuel Bellamy was only a pirate for a year, becoming captain after his mentor Benjamin Hornigold was voted out by the rest of the crew because he wouldn't attack the British. In the months that followed, Black Sam (so called because of the wigs he wore) went on to become perhaps the highest earning pirate of all time, capturing over 50 ships and netting a horde worth about £150 million in today's money before he was lost in a storm. The wreck of his

BATTEN DOWN THE HATCHES

Now meaning to prepare for pending trouble generally, the nautical term was used when a ship was about to enter rough seas and the captain would order his crew to batten down the hatches. These hatches were covered with tarpaulin edged with wooden strips (known as battens) to prevent them from blowing off.

ship was discovered in 1984 with copious treasure still on board.

EDWARD LOWE (1690-1724)

Though Ned Lowe began his criminal career as a lowly pickpocket he ended up becoming one of the most feared pirates of them all. He kept a collection of flags from various countries on board his ship and then flew the national flag of the vessel he wanted to attack so that its crew wouldn't suspect anything until it was too late. Excessively cruel, his tortures included cutting ears and heads off, disembowellings and tying ropes between his prisoners' fingers before setting fire to them. Legend has it that he once cut off a captain's lips, cooked them and made him eat them. Even his own men feared his wrath.

BLACK BART (1682-1722)

Bartholomew Roberts was a conventional sailor until he was captured by pirates and forced to become part of their crew. He ended up captain six weeks later. While only a pirate for four years, he captured more than 400 ships in that time. Sometimes he offered them back to their captains if they gave him gold. When he seized a ship he asked the crew members how their commanding officers treated them, and harsh commanders suffered particularly nasty fates. Black Bart's personal flag was the skull and crossbones, which has now become synonymous with all pirates.

CALICO JACK (1682–1720), ANNE BONNY (1697–1721) AND MARY READ (1685–1721)

In piracy's doomed love story, Jack Rackham met Anne Bonny when she disguised herself as a man to serve on his pirate ship. She wasn't the only one either: also on board was Mary Read. Apart from Rackham, it's possible none of the rest of the crew knew there were two female pirates with them. Rackham sought the King's Pardon (whereby pirates who voluntarily surrendered and renounced piracy would not be

DEVIL TO PAY

Used today to describe a heavy price to pay, the nautical origin stems from when sailors had to caulk (or pay) the seams with hot tar between the planks of the deck to prevent leakage. The devil seam was the longest seam on a wooden ship and the most difficult to caulk.

executed) in 1719 but Bonny convinced him to return to piracy. All three were captured in 1720. Rackham was executed but Bonny and Read were both pregnant, so were spared death sentences. Rackham's most famous legacy remains his personal flag – a skull and crossed swords.

ZHENG YI SAO (1775-1844)

Piracy was usually a man's world, but if there was a queen of pirates it was undoubtedly Chinese pirate Zheng Yi Sao, also known as Ching Shih. Born into poverty in Guangzhou, she married a pirate captain in 1801, but only on the condition that he agree to share his power and wealth with her. When he died in 1807 she seized control of his pirate federation and grew it into an empire – at its height the Red Flag Fleet had hundreds of ships and tens of thousands of pirates were under her command. Zheng Yi Sao demanded total obedience

ROCK THE BOAT

These days the term usually comes with the word 'don't' in front of it, referring to not disturbing a situation and causing trouble. This term comes from the action of rocking the boat from side to side, which could cause it to capsize.

under penalty of death, but her strict rules also dictated that any crews captured were to be given the opportunity to join the pirates, and no women were to be harmed. Her fleet was so powerful it couldn't be stopped and was only disbanded when the Chinese government agreed to pardon the pirates. Retiring from piracy at 35, she lived peacefully for the rest of her days.

WRITERS ON THE SEA

· ·

HOMER

Early western writing on the sea depicted a site of heavenly judgement and destruction. As Noah contends with the great flood and Jonah the enormity of the whale, so Odysseus must conquer the Aegean if he is to reach home. In Homer's epic, Odysseus' voyage forces him to confront sirens, the sea monsters Scylla and Charybdis, and ultimately the depths of hell. Though divine forces intervene throughout *The Odyssey,* survival is reliant on the technical skill and adaptability of the voyager. The sea adventure narrative would rely on such heroics for centuries to come.

WILLIAM SHAKESPEARE

Much early modern English literature presents the sea as a site of human agency, pitted against divine and supernatural forces. The playwright William Shakespeare penned works in which the sea drives plots, defines characters, shapes story worlds and provides inspiration

for some of his most famous poetry, including 'Full Fathom Five' from *The Tempest*. In the song, Ariel tricks Ferdinand into believing his father has drowned by describing the changes wrought to his body by the sea.

> *Full fathom five thy father lies,*
> *Of his bones are coral made;*
> *Those are pearls that were his eyes,*
> *Nothing of him that doth fade*
> *But doth suffer a sea-change*
>
> *– William Shakespeare, The Tempest*

DANIEL DEFOE, LORD BYRON AND SAMUEL TAYLOR COLERIDGE

The early eighteenth century saw the publication of *The Life and Strange Surprizing Adventures of Robinson Crusoe, of York, Mariner*, a classic adventure narrative, the story of a man stranded on a desert island. Later in the same century, poets and writers of the Romantic era detached the oceans from human activity, writing instead of seas which were 'boundless, endless, and sublime – The image of eternity', as in Byron's 'Childe Harold's Pilgrimage'. The sea in Samuel Taylor Coleridge's 'The Rime of the Ancient Mariner' is infused with the supernatural. When the titular seafarer shoots an albatross, his ship falls prey to malevolent forces.

> *I closed my lids, and kept them close,*
> *And the balls like pulses beat;*
> *For the sky and the sea, and the sea and*
> *   the sky*
> *Lay like a load on my weary eye,*
> *And the dead were at my feet.*
>
> – Samuel Taylor Coleridge, 'The Rime of
> the Ancient Mariner'

HERMAN MELVILLE, JOSEPH CONRAD AND VICTOR HUGO

Herman Melville, Joseph Conrad and Victor Hugo adapted the sea adventure genre for a range of subjects. Melville's *Moby-Dick* explores the world of commercial whaling. Narrated by Ishmael, the story charts Captain

Ahab's quest for vengeance on the white whale who cost him his leg. Joseph Conrad's body of works, including *Lord Jim*, *Nostromo* and *Heart of Darkness* drew on his own seafaring experience to interrogate the psychology of shipboard life. Considered among the greatest of maritime authors, Conrad's oceans were described as wild places, apt 'to bring out the irrational'. In *Les Travailleurs de la Mer* (*Toilers of the Sea*), Victor Hugo presents a battle between man and nature, as the protagonist toils to rescue a steamship's engine from a dangerous reef, home to a fearsome octopus.

HAND OVER FIST

Today the phrase is used to describe making money with ease or doing a job fast and effortlessly but its rather literal nautical origin came from sailors tugging at lines as fast as they could, hand over fist, to trim sheets and raise sails.

ROBERT LOUIS STEVENSON, JULES VERNE, C.S. FORESTER AND PATRICK O'BRIAN

Robert Louis Stevenson's *Treasure Island* revelled in the romance of piracy while Jules Verne's *Twenty Thousand Leagues Under the Sea* seized on modern technology for a fantastical voyage beneath the waves. Later, C. S. Forester's Hornblower series and Patrick O'Brian's Master and Commander novels threw naval officers into the furnace of the Napoleonic Wars.

VIRGINIA WOOLF, ERNEST HEMINGWAY, KAMAU BRATHWAITE AND DEREK WALCOTT

Modern and contemporary authors and poets have continued to draw on the boundless possibilities of the sea as subject, symbol and metaphor. In Virginia Woolf's novel *To the Lighthouse*, the perpetual motion of the waves

> ## THREE SHEETS TO THE WIND
> *The meaning has not changed since its first appearance. If the three sails were loose and blowing about in the wind, then the sails would be flapping about and the boat would lurch like a drunken sailor.*

denotes the unending and irresistible passage of time. For Ernest Hemingway in *The Old Man and the Sea*, the fisherman's struggle with a giant fish is a means of philosophising the nature of mortality. Poet Kamau Brathwaite places the sea to the fore in his trilogy *The Arrivants*, as he reflects upon contemporary Caribbean identity and its origins. For Saint Lucian poet Derek Walcott, the sea is rich in its symbolic potential, operating as a gateway to ancestral traditions and as a 'vault' for Caribbean history: in both cases, an archive in which the horrors of the middle passage of the transatlantic slave trade are held.

YANN MARTEL, RUPI KAUR AND MORE

There is no sign as yet of the sea disappearing from the literary canon. Contemporary writers continue to find inspiration in the watery depths and shipboard quests with which the genre is synonymous. Literature of the sea is a regular feature of the Booker Prize shortlists, with Yann Martel's *Life of Pi* winning the 2002 competition. Popular poet Rupi Kaur incorporates sea imagery into many of her works, while novels such as *The Mermaid and Mrs Hancock*, *The Loney* and *The Essex Serpent* revel in the supernatural possibilities of maritime fiction.

COOKING
AT SEA
·················

The food and drink consumed at sea, while often uninspiring, became such a central part of life that it has influenced national cuisines, languages and cultures across the world. With options on board limited, new recipes were born of whatever ingredients were available locally, and nautical food also began to influence cuisine ashore.

ACTION STATIONS

The ability to cook safely at sea was a vital step in making long distance voyages. Ancient vessels, generally smaller and made of wood or animal hides, were flammable, and, without materials separating the fire from the hull, cooking on board was impossible. Early sea-farers would have carried cold, pre-prepared food for shorter trips, or made regular landfall to replenish supplies and cook over a fire.

Vessels dating from late antiquity show the first evidence of purpose-built galleys, with tiled floors and ceilings to protect from fire and chimneys to remove smoke. They used portable stoves constructed from metal trays, or permanent hearths. These were eventually replaced by iron stoves in the eighteenth century, providing a greater range of cooking options for baking, roasting, and boiling.

As the size of ships and travel for leisure increased in the twentieth century, facilities improved and expanded to meet the demands of passengers, who expected the level of choice and quality on offer at hotels on land. Ocean liners were equipped with separate galleys for different classes of travellers and sometimes had up to sixty chefs to cater for the thousands of passengers.

ALL HANDS ON DECK
Ship's cook was historically a low-status position. No training or qualification was needed, so the standard of meals was highly variable. Cooks were often older or injured sailors who could not manage other duties anymore. Food was so low on the agenda in the nineteenth century that, on ships carrying migrants to America and Australia, steerage passengers were expected to provide and cook their own food, without adequate equipment or additional rations in the event of delays. There were many reports of fights over access to the fire and of the crew putting out the fire for the evening, while passengers queued, waiting to cook.

In the late nineteenth century, food standards at sea came under societal pressure in the UK. The growth of passenger vessels providing higher quality food, combined with low recruitment rates, drove the successful demand for certification of cooks on merchant ships in 1906. Culinary schools appeared across the country, providing highly trained marine chefs able to meet the escalating demands of ocean liner passengers.

A SQUARE MEAL

Before the invention of canning and refrigeration, food at sea had to be stored for long periods in a range of weather conditions, usually in barrels or tanks. Fresh ingredients were obtained through fishing, keeping live animals, or, sometimes, growing fresh plants on deck.

The majority of meals, however, had to consist of ingredients that could be stored dry, pickled or salted to prevent decay.

In Europe and North America, naval rations consisted primarily of biscuit as a daily ration, with smaller quantities of salt beef, pork, mutton or cod, some hard cheeses and butter, porridge or oats, and peas or beans. Adding stronger flavours with vinegar, onions, curry powder, mustard powder or other spices could vastly improve the flavour of bland or rotting provisions.

Biscuit, 'hardtack' or 'biscotti', as it was known to medieval Mediterranean sailors, refers to a hard, dry bread of flour, water and salt, baked twice, which was widely consumed at sea. Biscuit formed the basis of most meals, crumbled or dipped into liquid to soften. It acquired weevils in storage and had to be tapped on a hard surface or held over hot liquid to remove them before eating.

Stews, pies and, later, curries were common
dishes on board a merchant ship. They could
mostly be cooked in one pot and could make
tough, dried meats and vegetables more palat-
able. Dishes like 'lobscouse' and 'sea pie', made
of steamed or baked layers of crumbled biscuit,
salt beef and onion and potato, if available, were
popular on northern and central European
ships.

Suet-based puddings, also known as 'duffs',
were common meat substitutes and desserts
and have inspired many of Britain's tradi-
tional puddings. The base was flour, suet and
water, and then variations were made by adding

different ingredients and boiling the dough in a bag. 'Jam Roly Poly', 'Spotted Dog' and 'Plum Duff' were popular options.

Peas were a central element in sailors' rations. Whole or split peas were dried for storage and had to be soaked for hours before use. *Cookery for Seamen* (1894) describes pease pudding, made with 1 lb of split peas, 2 oz raw salt pork, mint and a ¼ teaspoon of pepper, tied in a cloth and simmered for two hours. This could be eaten cold in slices, or reheated with salt pork or bacon. Peas could be replaced with local pulses; on ships based in the East Indies, the local substitute was known as 'dholl' or dhal.

FEELING GROGGY

The problem of what to drink at sea could have
deadly consequences and grew increasingly
urgent as ships travelled further into the open
ocean.

Fresh water was the ideal source of hydration,
but it was almost impossible to provide at sea.
In barrels or metal tanks it stagnated quickly.
Wine and beer featured prominently in shipboard provisions both in navies and merchant
services, as they stored somewhat better than
water, were safer to drink and provided additional, necessary, calories. Beer was likely much
weaker than it is today, at around 2–3% proof,

and was issued to Nelson's navy in rations of one gallon per day.

In shortages, beer could be substituted with a pint of wine or a half-pint of locally available spirits. This was dependent on location, from brandy in the Mediterranean, to arrack in the East Indies stations and rum in the West Indies. It is not surprising then that in the 1740s Admiral Vernon, known as 'Old Grog' for his wearing of a grosgrain silk cloak, ordered that rum rations were diluted to prevent excessive drunkenness. Grog became the name for the watered-down rum. Some form of 'grog' was still served in the Royal Navy until 1970.

In the US during Prohibition the sea became a means of accessing alcohol for the public. The law did not apply to foreign-registered vessels, which was exploited by thirsty American passengers, who apparently drank record quantities on board *Mauretania* in 1920. This opportunity was jumped on by enterprising passenger liners offering short, affordable 'booze cruises' to nearby locations without prohibition, fuelling huge growth in the wider tourism industry in cities like Havana.

DEARTH IN THE DEEP

Between the sixteenth and eighteenth centuries, it is estimated that scurvy, caused by chronic lack of vitamin C common in shipboard diets, killed more than two million sailors. It was more lethal to mariners than combat, accidents and other diseases combined. While anecdotal evidence of scurvy's cure had existed for centuries, it was widely ignored until James Lind, a ship's surgeon, made the first substantial study in the 1750s, identifying the curative benefits of citrus. The Royal Navy began including lime juice in official rations in 1795, which originally gave the British the nickname 'limeys' among American sailors.

The lack of dietary variety and the unpredictable conditions at sea meant that provisions often had to be improvised in order to survive. Ships carried fishing lines and reported not only catching and eating fish, but porpoises, turtles and sharks too. Penguin, albatross, seal, even dog and pony meat, were eaten by crews stranded in the Antarctic.

In the worst circumstances, shipwrecks and starvation often drove sailors to look to cannibalism for survival. The case of the *Mignonette* in 1884 challenged a widely-held maritime custom that sailors resorting to murder for sustenance would not be prosecuted. Two crew members were successfully tried for the murder, for consumption, of a 17-year-old cabin boy, though they only received sentences of 6 months' imprisonment, as opposed to the usual death sentence. Lack of food and drink at sea could have the most dire consequences for seafarers.

NAUTICAL MYTHS, LEGENDS AND SUPERSTITIONS

· ·

Sailors have long been a superstitious lot. For most of humanity's time traversing the seas, ocean-going has been an incredibly risky business. In the dark, hundreds of miles from shore, the imagination could easily run away with a nervous sailor. With so much out of their control, the little rules and rituals sailors adopted were a way to try to exert some influence over their fates.

THE BERMUDA TRIANGLE

In 1945, an entire squadron of US Air Force planes on exercise over the Bahamas disappeared, their last radio messages giving the impression the pilots had no idea where they were. When the search plane sent to look for them also apparently vanished without trace, the reputation of the Bermuda Triangle was destined only to grow.

However, much of that reputation has only emerged in retrospect. The idea of the Bermuda

Triangle wasn't first discussed until 1950 and it wasn't even given a name until writer Vincent Gaddis coined the term in an article for the magazine *Argosy* in 1964. After that, any mysterious incident or unexplained disappearance in the area has been attributed to this deadly phenomenon.

Joshua Slocum, the first man to sail single-handedly around the world (and thus a highly experienced sailor), sailed into it and was never seen again. The US Navy lost several ships in the area, including the USS *Cyclops* in 1918 (the largest loss of personnel outside combat in the Navy's history) and both the USS *Proteus* and USS *Nereus* during the Second World War.

Statistically, however, the area (the size and precise location of which is much disagreed upon) is no more or less dangerous than any other part of the ocean. It is one of the busiest shipping lanes in the world, but is also in a part of the world notorious for tropical storms, with the Gulf Stream running straight through it to carry away any wreckage.

Its connection to piracy since the 1600s meant it has long been established as a dangerous region to avoid, and its reputation today owes a lot to people paying a lot more attention to anything that happens there than in any other place on Earth.

SEA MONSTERS

The fevered imaginations of nervous sailors can be no better illustrated than by the veritable menagerie of sea monsters supposedly bedevilling those taking to sea. A case in point is the mermaid. These weren't the fairytale characters of Disney movies – sailors saw them as more akin to the sirens of Ancient Greek myth, attempting to lure the unwary seaman to his death. However, sightings were probably just of sea lions or manatees – a momentary glimpse

of a head in the water, then a second glance perhaps only catching a flick of a tail. The imagination did the rest.

Imagination truly ran – or sailed – away with the crew of HMS *Daedalus* in 1848. Sailing off the Cape of Good Hope, several sailors reported spotting a 60 ft (18.2 m) sea serpent in the water 200 yards away. What they likely witnessed was just the big head and mouth of a whale, but by the time it got reported in the press, most of the crew swore they had seen an entire long reptile swimming nearby. They were taking the 'iceberg principle' too far. Only a small proportion of an iceberg is above water – the most dangerous part is beneath the surface, where you can't see it. For the crew of the *Daedalus*, and all the others who claim to have spotted sea serpents throughout history, everything they feared beneath the surface was, in truth, only in their imaginations.

The kraken, meanwhile, was the formidable sea monster of antiquity, a giant octopus that surfaces beneath the hull, wraps its legs around the ship, then crushes it and sucks sailors into a whirlpool as it descends into the depths again. What sailors probably saw instead was a giant squid, the females of which can reach 45 ft (14 m) in length. They are an impressive (though rare) sight, but don't pose any danger to ships.

THE FLYING DUTCHMAN

Perhaps the worst thing any sailor could encounter at sea was the ghost ship, the *Flying Dutchman*. Appearing to float just above the surface, the ghost ship was said to be manned by a dead crew who could never go home and were destined to sail the oceans forever. It was usually spotted from far away, but the distance offered no protection – any crew who spotted it

would soon suffer great misfortune and never see land again.

That doesn't explain how word of the *Flying Dutchman's* significance spread, however, if everyone who saw it was supposed to have died not long after. Science offers a less exciting but still fascinating explanation for the

phenomenon. *Fata Morgana* is most common in the polar regions, but can happen anywhere where the water gets icy enough. The phenomenon is basically a mirage caused by a layer of warm air over cold air acting like a refracting lens. So, what sailors might think is a ship floating just above the horizon is actually one sailing just beyond it. Seeing it happen relies on two ships being in exactly the right places at the same time, which is unlikely, but not necessarily rare.

RULES FOR SEAFARING

- Don't change a vessel's name – the sea will think you are trying to don a disguise to escape its attention.
- Don't whistle at sea – the wind will hear you and consider it a challenge, so a storm will surely follow.

- Don't shoot any albatrosses – they have long been believed to be the souls of deceased sailors come back to watch over and protect a ship.
- Don't cut your hair or allow a drop of blood to fall into the water – once the sea has got a taste of you, it will come back for more.
- Don't mention your destination, just your heading – assuming you will ever get there will tempt fate.
- Don't sail in a green vessel – green is the colour of the land, which will make the sea angry and cause you to run aground.
- Don't set sail on a Friday – and definitely not on Friday 13th.
- Don't count any fish you catch before the end of the day – the sea will consider you covetous and you won't catch any more.

- Don't say the word 'pig' – don't evoke the idea of anything that was not thought able to swim.
- Don't take any plants or seeds aboard – they belong to the earth and will seek solid ground... which may be the seabed.
- Don't let a priest on board – fate will assume you are preparing for a funeral, and perhaps those of the entire crew.

- Don't kill a rat – they might be a pest on board, but they can sense impending danger, so if a rat abandons ship, follow it!

OVER A BARREL
This saying is used these days to indicate being in a severely compromised position – if someone has you 'over a barrel' you know things aren't going well. This nautical phrase began its life in the literal sense. Sailors could find themselves punished for misdeeds by being tied over the barrel of a cannon and whipped.

SIX
ESSENTIAL
NAUTICAL
KNOTS

. . . .

These are some of the most useful knots for sailors with a step-by-step guide on how to tie them and what they are used for. They are commonly used on yachts and dinghies to help control sails and tie boats up to quaysides, pontoons, or tow boats.

FIGURE OF EIGHT

This is known as a 'stopper knot' as it prevents a length of rope passing through a block or cleat when you don't want it to. It is commonly used on the main sheet and jib sheet (sheet being the name of the rope used to control the sails) so that you don't lose the end of the rope.

1. Hold the rope out in one hand with one end in your other hand.
2. Pass the end over the top of the rope to create a loop (or face).
3. Now pass the end under the rope in your hand that is away from the loop, creating an 'S' shape.
4. Bring the end of the rope back over itself on the loop.
5. Pass the end of the rope through the loop.
6. Pull tight. It will now look like the number '8'.

Remember: make a face (the loop), strangle it (pass the rope around the back), poke it in the eye (and down the loop).

REEF KNOT

Historically this knot was used when the sails were reefed (made smaller) by gathering up the bottom of the sail using ropes passed through it at regular intervals. The ends of each rope were then tied together to keep the bottom of the sail rolled up in heavy weather. A reefed vessel is safer to sail in strong winds.

1. Take an end of the rope in each hand.
2. Pass the left end over the right end and under so that it twists out on top, just like the first step of tying a shoelace.
3. Then pass the end now on the right over the left and under.
4. When pulled together the knot should be symmetrical and tidy. The rope should come out on the top or on the bottom at each end of the knot.
5. If not, then you have tied a 'Granny Knot' where the knot is not symmetrical.

Remember: left over right and under, right over left and under.

ROUND TURN & TWO HALF HITCHES

This knot is used for tying up boats when the knot needs to be untied while the rope is still under some pressure. It is useful for tying around posts or rings.

1. Pass one end of the rope through or around an object, like a pole or ring.
2. Pass it around again without crossing it over the first turn to create the 'round turn'.
3. Take the long end of the rope (the 'standing part) in one hand and the shorter end that was passed around the pole (enough to complete the knot) in the other.
4. Now take the shorter end and wrap it around the 'standing part' of the rope, passing the end through the loop you have just made to create the first half hitch.
5. Repeat step 4 to create the second half hitch.

Remember: the two half hitches need to be tied in the same direction so that the ends come out on opposite sides.

CLOVE HITCH

The clove hitch is a good knot for securing a boat to a railing, post or similar object for the short term. It is not as secure as a round turn and two half hitches.

1. Pass the end of the rope over the post (or similar) and back round, crossing over the other end of the rope.
2. Continue to take the end of the rope over the post loosely, creating a loop.
3. Pass the end of the rope round the back of the post and through the loop.
4. Pull tight.

Remember: as with the round turn & two half hitches, the clove hitch (or two half hitches) needs to have the diagonal over the two turns.

KNOWING THE ROPES

'Knowing the ropes' or 'learning the ropes' is a phrase most often heard during a new job, when you are trying to pick up new skills and principles. The origin of this saying comes from sailors who had to memorise the function of the many miles of ropes in the rigging. It took an experienced sailor to know them all.

BOWLINE

This is an excellent knot if you do not want it to come undone, as it does not slip easily. It is useful for towing another boat or tying two bits of rope together instead of using a sheet bend.

1. Hold the length of rope in one hand and using your other hand, part of the way up the rope from the end, create a small loop by twisting the rope over itself. Clamp the rope at the twist with your thumb to stop it from falling out.
2. Next, bring the end of the rope up through the small loop from behind.
3. Take it around the back of the rope above your small loop, creating a larger loop below it.
4. When you have brought enough of the rope through the small loop and around the back of the rope, pass the end down through the small loop again.
5. Pull the rope tight above the small loop and the two ends of the rope passed through the small loop.

Remember: create the rabbit hole (the loop) then the rabbit (end of rope) comes out of the hole, goes around the tree and then heads back down the hole again.

DOUBLE SHEET BEND

This is a stronger and more secure knot than a single sheet bend. It is used to join two pieces of rope together, especially if they are different thicknesses, instead of using a bowline.

1. Create a 'U' shape in a piece of rope. This is called a 'bight'.
2. Pass the end of the second piece of rope up through the bight from underneath.
3. Continue to pass the rope around the back of the two ends of the first piece of rope.
4. Then pass the end of that rope under itself where it came up from below the bight. This has created a single sheet bend if you pull it tight now.
5. However, a double sheet bend includes the second piece of rope completing another turn around the back of the bight and back under itself like the first time.
6. Pull tight.

LIST OF CONTRIBUTORS
· ·

Andrew Choong

Kimberley
Cumberbatch

Lucy Dale

Jonathan Eyers

Alex Grover

Louise Macfarlane

Jeremy Michell

Aimee Mook

Kaori Nagai

Hannah Stockton

Victoria Syrett